Acknowledgements

The compilers and the publishers wish to thank the following for permission to use copyright material:

George Allen & Unwin, for *Oliphaunt*, from 'The Adventures of Tom Bombadil' by J. R. R. Tolkien.

Spike Milligan, for *Hello Mr. Python* and *Tell Me Little Woodworm*.

Greenwillow Books (A division of William Morrow & Company), for *The Porcupine* and *The Hippopotamus* by Jack Prelutsky, from 'Zoo Doings'. Copyright © 1970, 1983 by Jack Prelutsky.

Laurence Pollinger Ltd. and the Estate of the late Mrs. Freda Lawrence, for an extract from *Snake* by D. H. Lawrence.

Faber and Faber Ltd., for *The Lizard*, *The Bat* and an extract from *The Meadow Mouse*, from 'The Collected Poems of Theodore Roethke'.

Gerald Duckworth & Co. Ltd., for *The Yak* and *The Dodo*, from 'Complete Verse' by Hilaire Belloc.

Jean Kenward, for *Hedgehog*, *Bat*, *Mister Worm*, *Dragonfly* and *Gerbil*.

The Literary Executor of Leonard Clark, for *Hedgehog* by Leonard Clark.

Dobson Books Limited and the Literary Executor of Leonard Clark, for *Mouse and Kestrel* from 'Collected Poems and Verses for Children' by Leonard Clark.

Ian Serraillier, for *Anne and the Field-mouse*, © 1963 Ian Serraillier.

The Society of Authors on behalf of the copyright owner, Mrs. Iris Wise, for *The Snare* by James Stephens.

The Estate of the Hon. V. Sackville-West, for *The Greater Cats*.

Oxford University Press, for *The King* from 'Sjambok and Other Poems from Africa' by Douglas Livingstone. © Oxford University Press 1964. Also for *The Bear* by Frederick Brown from 'Every Man Will Shout' edited by Roger Mansfield and Isobel Armstrong, © Oxford University Press 1964.

St. John's College, Oxford and The Hogarth Press Ltd., for *The Panther*, from 'Selected Poems' by R. M. Rilke, translated by J. B. Leishman.

Jonathan Cape Ltd., for *Giraffe* by Carson McCullers, from 'Sweet as a Pickle and Clean as a Pig'.

Douglas Gibson, for *Falcon*, *Bluetit*, *Bumble-Bee* and *Tortoises*.

Martin Secker & Warburg Ltd., for *The Eagle* by T. W. H. Crosland.

Mrs. A. M. Walsh, for *The Blackbird* and *Goldfish* by John Walsh.

The Countryman, for *Swallows Over the South Downs* by Mary Holden, and for *Black Lamb* by Eleanor Glenn Wallis.

Rex Warner, for *Mallard*.

Leslie Norris, for *Swan*.

Curtis Brown Ltd., New York, for *Vulture* by X. J. Kennedy. © 1975 by X. J. Kennedy.

Harcourt Brace Jovanovich, Inc., for *Worms and the Wind*, from 'The Complete Poems of Carl Sandburg', copyright 1950 by Carl Sandburg; renewed 1978 by Margaret Sandburg, Helga Sandburg Crile and Janet Sandburg.

Odette Tchernine, for *The Gnats*.

Zoe Bailey, for *Ant* and *Dolphins*.

Basil Dowling, for *Spider*.

Stanley Cook, for *Tadpoles*, from 'Come Along', published by the author, 600 Barnsley Road, Sheffield, S5 6UA.

Norman MacCaig and The Hogarth Press Ltd., for *Frogs*, from 'Surroundings' by Norman MacCaig, and for *Fetching Cows*, from 'Measures' by Norman MacCaig.

Tom Earley and Chatto and Windus Ltd., for *Tiddlers*, from 'The Sad Mountain' by Tom Earley.

Russell M. Howell, for *Goldfish*.

The Lord Alfred Douglas Literary Estate, for *The Shark*.

Brian Carter, for *Otter*.

William Jay Smith, for *Seal*, from 'Laughing Time; Nonsense Poems', published 1980 by Seymour Lawrence/Belacorte, copyright © 1957, 1980 by William Jay Smith.

Aileen Fisher, for *Upside Down* and *My Puppy*, from 'Up the Windy Hill', published by Abelard-Schuman Ltd., New York, 1953, copyright renewed 1981.

The Literary Estate of Irene McLeod and Chatto and Windus Ltd., for *Lone Dog* by Irene McLeod, from 'Songs to Save a Soul', published by Chatto and Windus Ltd.

Olwyn Hughes, for *Roger the Dog* by Ted Hughes, from 'A First Poetry Book' by John Foster, published by Oxford University Press. Copyright Ted Hughes 1979.

Penguin Books Ltd., for *Bad Dog* by Brian Lee, from 'Late Home' by Brian Lee (p. 11), published by Kestrel Books, 1976. Copyright © 1976 by Brian Lee.

Gregory Harrison, for *Yellow Cat*, from 'The Night of the Wild Horses', published by Oxford University Press.

Mary Rayner, for *Fat Cat*.

Eve Merriam, for *The Stray Cat*, from 'Catch A Little Rhyme' by Eve Merriam, published by Atheneum. Copyright © 1966 by Eve Merriam. Reprinted by permission of the author.

Doubleday & Company Inc., for *The Tom-Cat*, copyright 1917 by The Sun Printing and Publishing Association, from the book 'Poems and Portraits' by Don Marquis.

David Higham Associates Ltd., for *Tropical Fish* by Christopher Hassall, from 'Here Be Lions' published by Cambridge University Press. Also for *Ladybird* by Clive Sansom, from 'Poetry Pack 1', published by Macmillan, London and Basingstoke. Also for *Cats* by Eleanor Farjeon, from 'Silver Sand and Snow', published by Michael Joseph.

Acknowledgements

Punch, for *I Had a Hippopotamus* by Patrick Barrington

Macmillan, London and Basingstoke, for *Cow* from 'Brownjohn's Beasts' by Alan Brownjohn.

The Estate of the late Dr. Alfred Noyes, for *Dobbin*, from 'Collected Poems' by Alfred Noyes, published by William Blackwood.

Atheneum Publishers, Inc., for *When Dinosaurs Ruled the Earth* by Patricia Hubbell, from 'The Apple Vendor's Fair'. Copyright © 1963 by Patricia Hubbell (New York: Atheneum 1963).

Edward Lowbury, for *The Monster*, from 'Green Magic' by Edward Lowbury.

H. A. C. Evans, for *The Brontosaurus*.

Curtis Brown Ltd., London, on behalf of The Estate of Ogden Nash, for *The Abominable Snowman* by Ogden Nash; and on behalf of John Wain for an extract from *Au Jardin des Plantes*, © John Wain 1961.

William Heinemann Ltd., for an extract from *The Hippocrump*, from Prefabulous Animiles' by James Reeves.

The Hamlyn Publishing Group Limited, for *Wyvern* and *Werewolf* by Charles Connell.

Ruth Skilling, for *Full Circle*.

James Hurley, for *Greedy Dog*.

Donald D. Derrick, Executor to the Estate of Miss Margaret Stanley-Wrench, and Dr. Robert Gittings, Literary Executor, for *Circus*, by Margaret Stanley-Wrench.

We have been unable to trace the copyright owners of the following poems and should be pleased to hear from them or their heirs and assigns. In the meantime, we venture to include:

An extract from *My Yellow Friend* by James Fenton; *Pigeons* by Richard Kell; *Wild Geese* by Berta Lawrence; *The Poor Snail* by J. M. Westrup; *The Hairy Dog* by Herbert Asquith; *Cat* by Mary Britton Miller; *On a Cat, Ageing* by Alexander Gray; *Tortoise* by David Speechley; *The Hens* by Elizabeth Madox Roberts; *The Marrog* by R. C. Scriven.

ANTHOLOGY

Poetry Plus

ve

THE POETRY LIBRARY

Schofield & Sims Ltd.   Huddersfield.

4/9/90

0 7217 0432 8

First Printed 1982
Reprinted 1983, 1984, 1985, 1988

Poetry Plus is a series of five books:

Book 1   0 7217 0431 X
Book 2   0 7217 0432 8
Book 3   0 7217 0433 6
Book 4   0 7217 0434 4
Book 5   0 7217 0435 2

Foreword

One of the aims of *Poetry Plus* is to stimulate children to write
their own poems. To encourage this, each section begins with
a series of thought-provoking questions and relevant vocabulary.
In addition, each provides ideas for inter-related topic work
which should promote higher reading skills and simple research.

Poetry Close-up pages consider individual poems and related
interest areas.

The poems have been carefully selected for variety and quality
and are grouped so that immediate interests and enthusiasms can
be pursued.

We hope that children will enjoy reading and listening to the
poems in *Poetry Plus* and that the series will encourage them to
write creatively.

Typeset in England by H Charlesworth & Co Ltd, Huddersfield
Printed in England by Henry Garnett & Co Ltd, Rotherham.

Contents

Contents

Contents

Creatures Real and Make-Believe

Hurt No Living Thing

Hurt no living thing;
Ladybird, nor butterfly,
Nor moth with dusty wing.
Nor cricket chirping cheerily,
Nor grasshopper so light of leap,
Nor dancing gnat, nor beetle fat,
Nor harmless worms that creep.

CHRISTINA ROSSETTI

World Wildlife

"When the lion roars in the jungle
The moisture shakes from the trees."

In this section you will find some poets' thoughts on creatures found in many distant places. Read the poems and think about these questions.

How do animals live in the wild?

.... Think of —prowling lions .... chattering monkeys .... hissing snakes .... silent, still crocodiles .... charging rhinos .... trampling elephants .... squawking exotic birds.

What are the different conditions around the world?

.... Think of —steaming forests .... dense undergrowth .... dusty plains .... arid deserts .... freezing ice floes .... cold snow-covered lands.

If you wish to write your own poem, these words may help you.

prairie	alert	savanna	territory	horizon	migrate
survive	flee	arctic	poisonous	scavenger	alarm
parched	freedom	sweltering	carnivorous	tropical	drought
fight	vast	graze	herd	attack	polar
waterhole	tundra	bathe	threaten	natural	protect

Animal Study

Write about four animals.
Choose two from each list ....

a) elephant .... monkey .... camel .... giraffe;
b) penguin .... polar bear .... seal .... arctic fox.

Draw a map which shows where in the world each can be found. What type of environment do they live in? What do they eat?

If you turn to page 15 you will find some questions on the poems themselves and some more things to do.

Oliphaunt

Grey as a mouse,
Big as a house,
Nose like a snake,
I make the earth shake,
As I tramp through the grass;
Trees crack as I pass.
With horns in my mouth
I walk in the South,
Flapping big ears.
Beyond count of years
I stump round and round,
Never lie on the ground,
Not even to die.
Oliphaunt am I,
Biggest of all,
Huge, old, and tall.
If ever you'd met me,
You wouldn't forget me.
If you never do,
You won't think I'm true;
But old Oliphaunt am I,
And I never lie.

J.R.R. TOLKIEN

from **My Yellow Friend**

When the lion roars in the jungle
The moisture shakes from the trees
And the swift invisible hummingbirds
Rustle in the scented breeze

And the slimey snakes slip silently
From the green sun-dappled grass
And the beasts retreat from the forest glade
To watch the lion pass.

JAMES FENTON

Hello Mr Python

Hello Mr Python
Curling round a tree,
Bet you'd like to make yourself
A dinner out of me

Can't you change your habits
Crushing people's bones?
I wouldn't like a dinner
That emitted fearful groans.

SPIKE MILLIGAN

11

The Porcupine

The porcupine is puzzled
that his friends should act so queer,
for though they come to visit him
they never come too near.

They often stop to say hello
and pass the time of day,
but still the closest of them
stays many feet away.

He sits and ponders endlessly,
but never finds a clue
to why his close companions
act the distant way they do.

The porcupine has never had
the notion in his brain
that what he finds enjoyable
to others is a pain.

JACK PRELUTSKY

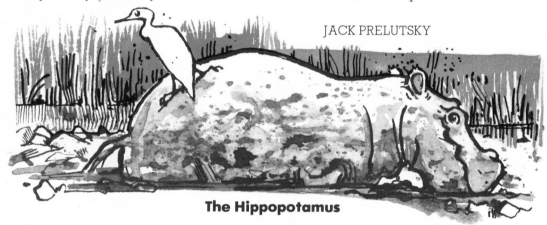

The Hippopotamus

The huge hippopotamus hasn't a hair
on the back of his wrinkly hide;
he carries the bulk of his prominent hulk
rather loosely assembled inside.

The huge hippopotamus lives without care
at a slow philosophical pace,
as he wades in the mud with a thump and a thud
and a permanent grin on his face.

JACK PRELUTSKY

The Yak

As a friend to the children commend me the Yak.
   You will find it exactly the thing:
It will carry and fetch, you can ride on its back,
   Or lead it about with a string.

The Tartar who dwells on the plains of Thibet
   (A desolate region of snow)
Has for centuries made it a nursery pet,
   And surely the Tartar should know!

Then tell your papa where the Yak can be got,
   And if he is awfully rich
He will buy you the creature — or else he will not.
   (I cannot be positive which.)

HILAIRE BELLOC

from Snake

A snake came to my water-trough

. . . .

He reached down from a fissure in the earth-wall
   in the gloom
And trailed his yellow-brown slackness soft-bellied
   down, over the edge of the stone trough
And rested his throat upon the stone bottom,
And where the water had dripped from the tap, in
   a small clearness,
He sipped with his straight mouth,
Softly drank through his straight gums, into his
   slack long body,
Silently.

THE POETRY LIBRARY

D.H. LAWRENCE

The Lizard

He too has eaten well —
I can see that by the distended pulsing middle;
And his world and mine are the same,
The Mediterranean sun shining on us, equally,
His head, stiff as a scarab, turned to one side,
His right eye staring straight at me,
One leaf-like foot hung laxly
Over the worn curb of the terrace,
The tail straight as an awl,
Then suddenly flung up and over,
Ending curled around and over again,
A thread-like firmness.

(Would a cigarette disturb him?)

At the first scratch of the match
He turns his head slightly,
Retiring to nudge his neck half-way under
A dried strawberry leaf,
His tail grey with the ground now,
One round eye still toward me.
A white cabbage-butterfly drifts in,
Bumbling up and around the bamboo windbreak;
But the eye of the tiny lizard stays with me.
One greenish lid lifts a bit higher,
Then slides down over the eye's surface,
Rising again, slowly,
Opening, closing.

To whom does this terrace belong? —
With its limestone crumbling into fine greyish dust,
Its bevy of bees, and its wind-beaten rickety sun-chairs.
Not to me, but this lizard,
Older than I, or the cockroach.

THEODORE ROETHKE

14

Poetry Close-up

1. Which phrase in 'Oliphaunt' is used by J.R.R. Tolkien instead of 'very old'?

2. The description of the snake by James Fenton is actually quite wrong. Can you say why?

3. Friends of 'The Porcupine' do not go too near him. Can you say why?

4. In 'The Hippopotamus' two different words are used to describe his size. Which are they?

5. Who has made a pet out of 'The Yak'?

6. From 'The Lizard' by Theodore Roethke, list words and phrases which suggest the terrace in the poem is many years old.

7. Write a story entitled 'Lost in the Jungle' — describe your journey, the animals you meet and your adventures.

Other Things To Do

.... What is a safari park?

.... What is a game reserve?

.... Draw a map of Africa showing forests and deserts.

.... Explain how the camel is adapted for living in the desert. Can you find any more animals that have become adapted to difficult conditions?

.... Today many species of animals are in danger of becoming extinct. Can you find out the names of some of these and where they live? What can we do to save them?

British Wildlife

"Among the taller wood with ivy hung,
The old fox plays and dances round her young."

In this section you will find some poets' thoughts
on wild creatures found in Britain. Read the poems
and think about these questions.

How do creatures behave in the countryside?

. . . Think of —skulking foxes . . . . scurrying rabbits
. . . . scampering squirrels . . . . timid
deer . . . . burrowing moles . . . .
shuffling hedgehogs.

How do we treat our wildlife?

. . . . Think of —captive animals . . . . blood sports . . . .
animals as pests . . . . polluted waters
. . . . conservation.

Is some of our wildlife rarely seen?

. . . . Think of —hidden otters . . . . coiled snakes . . . .
shy badgers . . . . secretive pine
martens . . . . furtive wild cats.

If you wish to write your own poem, these words may help you.

species	chase	camouflage	extinct	conserve	diurnal
timid	native	breed	habitat	enemy	trap
nocturnal	survive	playful	predator	hunt	agile
prey	docile	gentle	rodent	vermin	gnaw

Wildlife Worksheet

Choose two common creatures and two rare
creatures from Britain's wildlife . . . .

Draw each one and then write about . . . .
where they live . . . . what they eat . . . . their usual or
unusual habits . . . . do the parents or young have special
names? Find out as much as you can about each one.

If you turn to page 22 you will find some questions
on the poems themselves and some more things to do.

Whisky Frisky

Whisky Frisky,
Hipperty hop,
Up he goes
To the tree top!

Whirly, twirly,
Round and round,
Down he scampers
To the ground.

Furly, curly,
What a tail,
Tall as a feather,
Broad as a sail.

Where's his supper?
In the shell.
Snappy, cracky,
Out it fell.

ANON.

Hedgehog

Listen —
Old Snuffler's in the grass
circling
his nightly track —
dark in the starlight,
round and shy
with prickles on his back,
sniffing and rustling
as he goes
on tiny, hurrying feet
with shifting eye
and eager nose
searching for food
to eat;
beetles, and berries
red or black,
worms,
secret wriggling things,
a bite of this . . . .
a taste of that . . . .
Sometimes,
somebody brings
a saucerful
of milk and bread —
how sweet that is to sup!
Listen —
Old Hedgehog's in the grass
gobbling
his supper up.

JEAN KENWARD

Hedgehog

Comes out by day in autumn,
exploring hedgehog, betrays himself
snoring loudly in leafy ditch;
plump with summer's fat, moves along,
battering slow way through dry twigs.
I hear him lumbering, hairy head appears,
then all his ten-inch prickly length,
makes for the bank, senses me there,
rolls into a ball, waits for the attack.
I leave him alone though, curled up on the hill's lip,
this earth-brown savage, enemy of frogs.
He'll chew beetles and mice to powder, hear
every small noise in undergrowth,
will take on snakes by the tail,
bayonet them with needle-spines.
Shy of the sun, dislikes company,
cannot see far, a fine swimmer,
drinks milk.

LEONARD CLARK

The Squirrel

The squirrel, flippant, pert, and full of play,
Drawn from his refuge in some lonely elm
That age or injury hath hollowed deep,
Where, on his bed of woodland matted leaves,
He has out-slept the winter, ventures forth
To frisk awhile, and bask in the warm sun:
He sees me, and at once, swift as a bird,
Ascends the neighbouring beech: there whisks his
    brush,
And perks his ears, and stamps and cries aloud,
With all the prettiness of feigned alarm,
And anger insignificantly fierce.

WILLIAM COWPER

18

Bat

Did you see?
  Did you see
what I saw?
  Look — a bat
like a bit of burn't paper
  lop-sided and flat
flicking into the night . . . .
  Here he comes
yet once more . . . .
  Did you see?
Did you hear?
  He was calling, before,
in a voice
  that was high
as a steeple —
  so small
that you hardly could hear
  what he signalled
at all.
  Did you see?
Did you see
  what I saw?
Look — again,
  a mysterious something
as dark
  as a stain
flaking out of the night
  first this way
and then that.
  Did you see?
Did you see
  what I saw?
Look —
  a bat!   JEAN KENWARD

The Bat

By day the bat is cousin to the mouse.
He likes the attic of an aging house.

His fingers make a hat about his head.
His pulse beat is so slow we think him dead.

He loops in crazy figures half the night
Among the trees that face the corner light.

But when he brushes up against a screen,
We are afraid of what our eyes have seen;

For something is amiss or out of place
When mice with wings can wear a human face.

THEODORE ROETHKE

19

Anne and The Field-mouse

We found a mouse in the chalk quarry today
In a circle of stones and empty oil drums
By the fag ends of a fire. There had been
A picnic there; he must have been after the crumbs.

Jane saw him first, a flicker of brown fur
In and out of the charred wood and chalk-white.
I saw him last, but not till we'd turned up
Every stone and surprised him into flight.

Though not far — little zigzag spurts from stone
To stone. Once, as he lurked in his hiding-place,
I saw his beady eyes uplifted to mine.
I'd never seen such terror in so small a face.

I watched, amazed and guilty. Beside us suddenly
A heavy pheasant whirred up from the ground,
Scaring us all; and, before we knew it, the mouse
Had broken cover, skimming away without a sound,

Melting into the nettles. We didn't go
Till I'd chalked in capitals on a rusty can:
THERE'S A MOUSE IN THOSE NETTLES. LEAVE
HIM ALONE. NOVEMBER 15TH. ANNE.

IAN SERRAILLIER

The Snare

I hear a sudden cry of pain!
　There is a rabbit in a snare:
Now I hear the cry again,
　But I cannot tell from where.

But I cannot tell from where
　He is calling out for aid;
Crying on the frightened air,
　Making everything afraid.

Making everything afraid,
　Wrinkling up his little face,
As he cries again for aid;
　And I cannot find the place!

And I cannot find the place
　Where his paw is in the snare:
Little one! Oh, little one!
　I am searching everywhere.

JAMES STEPHENS

The Vixen

Among the taller wood with ivy hung,
The old fox plays and dances round her young.
She snuffs and barks if any passes by
And swings her tail and turns prepared to fly.
The horseman hurries by, she bolts to see,
And turns agen, from danger never free.
If any stands she runs among the poles
And barks and snaps and drives them in the holes.
The shepherd sees them and the boy goes by
And gets a stick and progs the hole to try.
They get all still and lie in safety sure,
And out again when everything's secure,
And start and snap at blackbirds bouncing by
To fight and catch the great white butterfly.

JOHN CLARE

Poetry Close-up

1. In the poem 'Whisky Frisky', which animal is being talked about and what do you think he will eat for his supper?

2. Leonard Clark writes in 'Hedgehog' that he hears him lumbering. What do you think gives the creature away?

3. In 'Bat' by Jean Kenward, what do you think it is about this creature which leads to it being described as 'a bit of burn't paper'?

4. Find a sentence from Theodore Roethke's poem 'The Bat' which proves the creature to be nocturnal.

5. In the poem by Ian Serraillier, can you list the evidence which suggests some people do not care for the countryside?

6. In John Clare's poem, what are the dangers to the vixen and her cubs?

7. Imagine you find an injured animal. Write the story of how you care for it and strike up a friendship.

Other Things To Do

1. Find out about the National Trust.

2. What is myxomatosis? What effects has it had?

3. Find out about the tracks and signs made by wild creatures.

4. Make a list of sayings based on wildlife, such as 'cunning as a fox' — 'wise as an owl'.

5. Read 'Tarka the Otter' by Gavin Maxwell and 'Watership Down' by Richard Adams.

Captive Animals

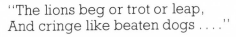

"The lions beg or trot or leap,
And cringe like beaten dogs ...."

In this section you will find some poets' thoughts on animals in captivity. Read the poems and think about these questions on the pleasure you might get, but the sadness you might feel, when you see a caged animal.

Why do you enjoy looking at animals from around the world?

.... Think of —multicoloured birds .... agile monkeys .... lumbering elephants .... padding tigers .... performing seals .... still, silent snakes.

Do any of the animals make you feel sad?

.... Think of —caged birds .... sad-eyed monkeys .... weary elephants .... bored tigers .... frustrated seals .... captive snakes.

If you wish to write your own poem, these words may help you.

supple	roar	despair	ferocious	wearisome	savage
strength	active	sullen	surly	powerful	fierce
graceful	miserable	menace	howl	vigorous	bellow
gentle	downcast	nimble	screech	timid	prowl

Zoo-ology

What is zoo short for?

.... Find out about the zoos kept by ancient kings ....
When and where was the first English zoo opened? ....
Write about the formation of the London Zoo.

.... How are animals obtained for a zoo and how are they fed and kept in good health?

If you turn to page 30 you will find some questions on the poems themselves and some more things to do.

Captive Animals

Circus

Saucer of sand, the circus ring,
A cup of light, clowns tumbling.

Horses with white manes sleek and streaming,
Bits jingling, tinkling, silk skins gleaming.

But there, shut in their iron cage,
Sulky, drowsy, dulled by rage

The lions beg or trot or leap,
And cringe like beaten dogs, and creep,

King beasts, who should be free to run
Through forests striped with shade and sun,

With fierce, proud eyes and manes like fire.
These manes hang dull like rusty wire.

And when the trainer cracks his whip
They snarl and curl a sullen lip,

And only in their dreams are free
To crush and kill man's cruelty.

MARGARET STANLEY-WRENCH

The Greater Cats

The greater cats with golden eyes
Stare out between the bars.

Deserts are there, and different skies,
And night with different stars.

V. SACKVILLE-WEST

24

The King

Old Tawny's mane is moth-
eaten now, a balding monk's tonsure
and his fluid thigh muscles flop
slack as an exhausted boxer's;

Creaks a little and is
just a fraction under fast (he's lame)
in those last short lethal rushes
at the slim white-eyed winging game;

Can catch them still of course,
the horny old claws combing crimson
from the velvet flanks in long scores,
here in the game-park's environs;

Each year, panting heavily,
manages with aged urbanity
to smile full-faced and yellowly
at a thousand box cameras.

DOUGLAS LIVINGSTONE

The Panther

His gaze, going past those bars, has got so misted
with tiredness, it can take in nothing more.
He feels as though a thousand bars existed,
and no more world beyond them than before.

Those supple powerful paddings, turning there
in tiniest of circles, well might be
the dance of forces round a centre where
some mighty will stands paralyticly.

Just now and then the pupils' noiseless shutter
is lifted. — Then an image will indart,
down through the limbs' intensive stillness flutter,
and end its being in the heart.

R.M. RILKE

The Bear

His sullen shaggy-rimmed eyes followed my every
    move,
Slowly gyrating they seemed to mimic the movements
    of his massive head.
Similarly his body rolled unceasingly
From within.
As though each part possessed its own motion
And could think
And move for itself alone.
He had come forward in a lumbering, heavy spurt
Like a beer barrel rolling down a plank.
The tremendous volume of his blood-red mouth
Yawned
So casually
But with so much menace.
And still the eye held yours.
So that you had to stay.
And then it turned.
Away.
So slowly.
Back
With that same motion
Back
To the bun-strewn
And honey-smelling back of its cage.

FREDERICK BROWN

The Gorilla

The gorilla lay on his back,
One hand cupped under his head,
Like a man.

Like a labouring man, tired with work,
A strong man with his strength burnt away
In the toil of earning a living.

Only of course he was not tired out with work,
Merely with boredom: his terrible strength
All burnt away by prodigal idleness.

A thousand days, and then a thousand days,
Idleness licked away his beautiful strength,
He having no need to earn a living.

It was all laid on, free of charge.
We maintained him, not for doing anything,
But for being what he was.

And so that Sunday morning he lay on his back,
Like a man, like a worn-out man,
One hand cupped under his terrible hard head.

Like a man, like a man,
One of those we maintain, not for doing anything,
But for being what they are.

A thousand days, and then a thousand days,
With everything laid on, free of charge,
They cup their heads in prodigal idleness.

JOHN WAIN

Giraffe

At the zoo I saw: A long-necked, velvety Giraffe
Whose small head, high above the strawy,
   zoo-y smells
Seemed to be dreaming.
Was she dreaming of African jungles
   and African plains
That she would never see again?

CARSON McCULLERS

The Eagle

They have him in a cage
And little children run
To offer him well-meant bits of bun,
And very common people say, 'My word!
Ain't he a 'orrible bird!'
And the smart, 'How absurd!
Poor, captive, draggled,
              downcast lord of the air!'

Steadfast in his despair,
He doth not rage;
But with unconquerable eye
And soul aflame to fly,
Considereth the sun.

T.W.H. CROSLAND

Falcon

Below on the smooth greensward
Beyond the watching crowd
    The falconer waits,
Until at a sign the bird
Is released and straight
Sails on whispering wings
Through the sky's cool amethyst,
Down to the tempting bait
On the falconer's gloved wrist.

What a beauty is there
In the curve and turn and twist
Of fine bones and feathers like fur
    In the vibrant air!
But oh! in the glittering eyes,
In that rapier of a beak
Of this bird of prey
Trained to make sport for crowds,
What primitive hunger lurks
To darken some summer day,
A terrible vengeance take.

DOUGLAS GIBSON

Poetry Close-up

1. Read closely the poem 'Circus' by Margaret Stanley-Wrench. Why are the lions' manes like rusty wire and why do they have sullen lips?

2. In 'The King', Douglas Livingstone describes part of the lion as like 'a balding monk's tonsure'. What does he mean?
   In the same poem, why does the lion seem to smile at the box cameras?

3. Look at 'The Bear' by Frederick Brown.
   a) What does 'gyrating' mean?
   b) Why is the bear 'like a beer barrel rolling down a plank'?

4. Was the giraffe in Carson McCullers' poem born in the zoo?

5. In 'The Eagle', why do you think the eagle 'considereth the sun'?

6. Imagine a lion has escaped from a visiting circus. Describe how you help to recapture it.

Other Things To Do

1. Find out how animals are trained for a circus.

2. What is the difference between a zoo and a safari park? Write a letter to one of them asking for any information you might require.

3. What is zoology? How are animals named in a scientific way and what sort of work do zoologists do?

4. Read 'A Good Sixpenn'orth' from 'The Goalkeeper's Revenge' by Bill Naughton.

Birds

"He flew with a flash of blue
And primrose into the sun."

In this section you will find some poems about many different birds. Read the poems and then think about these questions.

How can you describe different kinds of birds?

.... Think of —strutting pigeons .... swooping swifts ....
brooding owls .... elegant swans ....
departing geese .... hovering kestrels
.... the majestic eagle.

Would you like to fly like a bird?

.... Think of —the panorama below .... sometimes of
traffic, dirt, noise and bustle ....
sometimes of meadows, lakes, woods
and solitude.

.... Think of —freedom .... soaring and gliding ....
silent loneliness .... battling through
the wind .... diving from the heights.

If you wish to write your own poem, these words might help you.

outspread	stare	beat	talons	plumage	colony
screech	soar	wade	formation	dabble	dart
swing	luminous	glow	migrate	territory	ascend
descend	surveying	hoot	buffeted	eaves	flight

Wingless Wonders

Some birds are unable to fly. These include the — emu, penguin, ostrich, kiwi and rhea.
Find out about these birds and draw them.

Some flightless birds have become extinct. These include the Dodo (see the poem) and the Great Auk. Where did these birds live? .... when did they become extinct and why?

If you turn to page 38 you will find some questions on the poems themselves and some more things to do.

The Blackbird

She builds her nest on a bare branch,
In reaching-distance from the ground,
And hopes the loosening hawthorn-buds
With their quick leaves will wrap her round.

See, down she drops to the pasture-field,
Tussling for grass in the hard earth.
Then back to her nest again. Her time
Is on her: her eggs cry out for birth.

But now an April storm blows up —
Three nights and days of freezing air —
Leafing's delayed; and there she sits,
Plain to all eyes, moping and bare.

Then comes a boy's rough hand. Then she,
Pushed out, and hopelessly looking on,
Sees with sad eyes her hard-won nest
Battered, her shining children gone.

JOHN WALSH

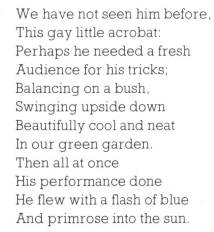

Bluetit

We have not seen him before,
This gay little acrobat:
Perhaps he needed a fresh
Audience for his tricks;
Balancing on a bush,
Swinging upside down
Beautifully cool and neat
In our green garden.
Then all at once
His performance done
He flew with a flash of blue
And primrose into the sun.

DOUGLAS GIBSON

Birds

Swallows Over The South Downs

England, we're here again,
Sleet-squalls and blinding rain
(All just as usual)
   Greet us on landing.
Head-winds through Italy,
Fog over Brittany,
Why we don't give it up 's
   Past understanding.

Buffeted, blown, half-dead ....
Hey, look, there's Beachy Head!
Green turf and milky-white
   Chalk-cliffs like Dover!
Sun-gleams at last, hurray!
.... I'm off down Uckfield way,
Country'll be looking grand
   Now the rain's over.

.... Primroses, blowing leaves,
Thatched roofs and cottage eaves,
Oast-houses, dusky-dark,
   What sites for nesting!
Come on, the fun's begun,
Hurry up, everyone,
Don't let's waste any time
   Preening and resting ....

MARY HOLDEN

Pigeons

They paddle with staccato feet
In powder-pools of sunlight,
Small blue busybodies
Strutting like fat gentlemen
With hands clasped
Under their swallowtail coats;
And, as they stump about,
Their heads like tiny hammers
Tap at imaginary nails
In non-existent walls.
Elusive ghosts of sunshine
Slither down the green gloss
Of their necks an instant, and are gone.

Summer hangs drugged from sky to earth
In limpid fathoms of silence:
Only warm dark dimples of sound
Slide like slow bubbles
From the contented throats.

Raise a casual hand —
With one quick gust
They fountain into air.

RICHARD KELL

Birds

Wild Geese

Over grey seas
The wild geese come,
Wild birds seeking
A winter home.

They fly all night,
Close to the sky,
Calling to the stars
Their strange, wild cry.

Where the cold tide creeps
In lines of foam,
To wild, windy marshes
The wild geese come.

BERTA LAWRENCE

Mallard

Squawking they rise from reeds into the sun,
climbing like furies, running on blood and bone,
with wings like garden shears clipping the misty air,
four mallard, hard-winged, with necks like rods
fly in perfect formation over the marsh.

Keeping their distance, gyring, not letting slip the air,
but leaping into it straight like hounds or divers,
they stretch out into the wind and sound their horns again.

Suddenly siding to a bank of air unbidden
by hand signal or morse message of command
down sky they plane, sliding like corks on a current,
designed so deftly that all air is advantage,

till, with few flaps, orderly as they left the earth,
alighting among curlew they pad on mud.

REX WARNER

Swan

Swan, unbelievable bird, a cloud floating,
Arrangement of enormous white chrysanthemums
In a shop kept by angels, feathery statue
Carved from the fall of snow,

You are not too proud to take the crusts I offer.
You are so white that clear water stains you,
And I am ashamed that you have to swim
Here, where cigarette cartons hang in the lake,

And the plastic containers that held our ice-cream.
Now you bend your neck strong as a hawser
And I see your paddles like black rubber
Open and close as you move the webs of your swimming.

About you the small ducks, the coots, and the timid
Water-rails keep their admiring distances. Do not hurry.
Take what you need of my thrown bread, white swan,
Before you drift away, a cloud floating.

LESLIE NORRIS

The Barn Owl

While moonlight, silvering all the walls,
Through every mouldering crevice falls,
Tipping with white his powdery plume,
As shades or shifts the changing gloom;
The Owl that, watching in the barn,
Sees the mouse creeping in the corn,
Sits still and shuts his round blue eyes
As if he slept — until he spies
The little beast within his stretch —
Then starts — and seizes on the wretch!

SAMUEL BUTLER

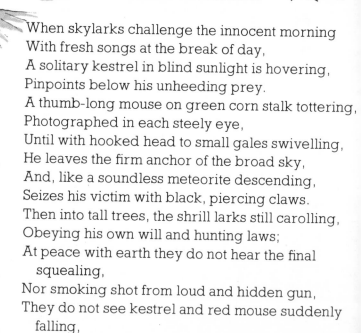

Mouse and Kestrel

When skylarks challenge the innocent morning
With fresh songs at the break of day,
A solitary kestrel in blind sunlight is hovering,
Pinpoints below his unheeding prey.
A thumb-long mouse on green corn stalk tottering,
Photographed in each steely eye,
Until with hooked head to small gales swivelling,
He leaves the firm anchor of the broad sky,
And, like a soundless meteorite descending,
Seizes his victim with black, piercing claws.
Then into tall trees, the shrill larks still carolling,
Obeying his own will and hunting laws;
At peace with earth they do not hear the final
    squealing,
Nor smoking shot from loud and hidden gun,
They do not see kestrel and red mouse suddenly
    falling,
Continue still blithe singing to the sun.

LEONARD CLARK

The Eagle

He clasps the crag with crooked hands
Close to the sun in lonely lands,
Ringed with the azure world, he stands.

The wrinkled sea beneath him crawls;
He watches from his mountain walls,
And like a thunderbolt he falls.

ALFRED, LORD TENNYSON

Vulture

The vulture's very like a sack
Set down and left there drooping.
His crooked neck and creaky beak
Look badly bent from stooping
Down to the ground to eat dead cows
So they won't go to waste,
Thus making up in usefulness
For what he lacks in taste.

X.J. KENNEDY

Poetry Close-up

1. Why is 'The Blackbird' by John Walsh a sad poem?

2. Mary Holden's poem is about 'migrating' swallows. What does this mean?

   In the same poem what does she mean by 'head-winds' and where in Britain is Beachy Head?

3. Read the poem 'Pigeons' by Richard Kell.
   a) What does he mean by 'staccato feet'?
   b) What does he mean by the 'elusive ghosts of sunshine'?

4. Read the poem 'Swan'. The poet compares it to three different things. What are they?

   In the same poem, why is the poet 'ashamed'?

5. In the poem 'Mouse and Kestrel', what happens to the kestrel?

6. Lord Tennyson has written about 'The Eagle'.
   a) What are the eagle's crooked hands?
   b) What colour is azure?
   c) Why does the sea look wrinkled?

Other Things To Do

1. Find out where your nearest bird reserve is and, if possible, visit it. One of the most famous in Britain is Slimbridge Can you discover where it is and who runs it?

2. Make a nesting box and a bird-table for your garden and then be an 'ornithologist' yourself with the help of some books.

3. What does R. S. P. B. stand for? Can you find out more about this organisation?

Insects, Snails and Worms

"The gnats are dancing in the sun,
In vibrant needles of light they run"

In this section, you will find some poets' thoughts on insects, snails and worms. Read the poems and think about these questions on the Earth's smallest creatures.

How do these tiny creatures live?

... Think of —worms .... in the deep, dark earth .... wriggling and twisting .... slithering and sliding .... hungry birds waiting.

... Think of —bees .... in flight .... bumbling and buzzing .... hovering over flowers .... laden with honey .... returning to the hive.

Are insects pleasant creatures?

... Think of —creepy-crawlies .... slimy slugs .... upturned stones .... colourful butterflies .... furry caterpillars.

If you wish to write your own poem, these words might help you.

dart	swarm	scurry	quiver	sluggish	drone
dive	writhe	flutter	delicate	fragile	hum
bright	squirm	antennae	pollen	camouflage	crawl

Insect Inquiry

Insects can be harmful or helpful to mankind.

Find out about —
.... the diseases that can be spread by ....
a mosquito .... a tsetse fly .... a louse .... a flea.
.... the damage caused by .... colorado and death-watch beetles .... locusts .... woodworm.

Find out about —
.... honey produced by bees .... the silkworm ....
lacquer-and-scale insects .... cochineal.

If you turn to page 46 you will find some questions on the poems themselves and some more things to do.

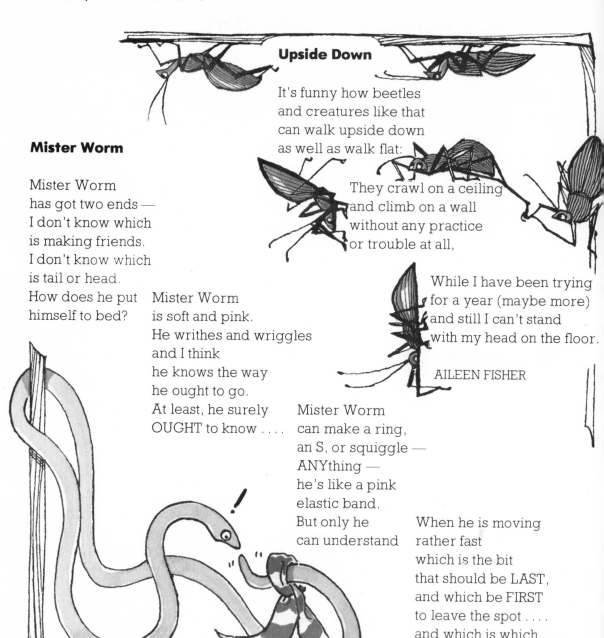

Upside Down

It's funny how beetles
and creatures like that
can walk upside down
as well as walk flat:

They crawl on a ceiling
and climb on a wall
without any practice
or trouble at all,

While I have been trying
for a year (maybe more)
and still I can't stand
with my head on the floor.

AILEEN FISHER

Mister Worm

Mister Worm
has got two ends —
I don't know which
is making friends.
I don't know which
is tail or head.
How does he put
himself to bed?

Mister Worm
is soft and pink.
He writhes and wriggles
and I think
he knows the way
he ought to go.
At least, he surely
OUGHT to know . . . .

Mister Worm
can make a ring,
an S, or squiggle —
ANYthing —
he's like a pink
elastic band.
But only he
can understand

When he is moving
rather fast
which is the bit
that should be LAST,
and which be FIRST
to leave the spot . . . .
and which is which . . . .
        and what is what . . . .

JEAN KENWARD

40

Worms and the Wind

Worms would rather be worms.
Ask a worm and he says, "Who knows what a worm
    knows?"
Worms go down and up and over and under.
Worms like tunnels.
When worms talk they talk about the worm world.
Worms like it in the dark.
Neither the sun nor the moon interest a worm.
Zigzag worms hate circle worms.
Curve worms never trust square worms.
Worms know what worms want.
Slide worms are suspicious of crawl worms.
One worm asks another, "How does your belly drag
    today?"
A straight worm says, "Why not be straight?"
Worms tired of crawling begin to slither.
Long worms slither farther than short worms.
Middle-sized worms say, "It is nice to be neither long
    nor short."
Old worms teach young worms to say, "Don't be
    sorry for me unless you have been a worm and
    lived in worm places and read worm books."
When worms go to war they dig in, come out again
    and fight, dig in again, come out and fight again, dig
    in again, and so on.
Worms underground never hear the wind
    underground and sometimes they ask, "What is this
    wind we hear of?"

CARL SANDBURG

The Poor Snail

The snail says, "Alas!"
And the snail says, "Alack!
Why must I carry
My house on my back?
You have a home
To go in and out,
Why must mine always be
Carried about?
Not any tables,
Not any chairs,
Not any windows,
Not any stairs,
Pity my misery,
Pity my wail —
For I must always be
Just a poor snail."
But he's terribly slow,
So perhaps it's as well
That his shell is his home,
And his home is his shell.

J.M. WESTRUP

Tell Me Little Woodworm

Tell me little woodworm
Eating thru the wood.
Surely all that sawdust
Can't do you any good.

Heavens! Little woodworm
You've eaten all the chairs
So *that's* why poor old Grandad's
Sitting outside on the stairs.

SPIKE MILLIGAN

Bumble-Bee

In his black and yellow
Striped jersey he moves slowly
From flower to flower
Sucking out the honey;
A fat and friendly fellow
Buzzing around me where
I am writing in the sun.

Before the house has awoken
And the Sunday rumbling
Of traffic has begun
The bumble-bee keeps bumbling
Among the flowers and tumbling
Drunk with honey
Round my table in the sun.

DOUGLAS GIBSON

Ladybird

Tiniest of turtles!
Your shining back
Is a shell of orange
With spots of black.

How trustingly you walk
Across this land
Of hairgrass and hollows
That is my hand.

Your small wire legs,
So frail, so thin,
Their touch is swansdown
Upon my skin.

There! break out
Your wings and fly:
No tenderer creature
Beneath the sky.

CLIVE SANSOM

The Gnats

The gnats are dancing in the sun,
In vibrant needles of light they run
On the air, and hover in noiseless sound,
Ecstasy ballet, round and around,
Soon for human body bound.

The pin-thin slivers, wingy, white,
Whirl in restless, passionate flight —
Zooming atoms circling, twisting,
Darting, jiving,
Target-diving.
In orbit on orbit of dazzle-gold light,
The gnats are limbering up to bite.

ODETTE TCHERNINE

Insects, Snails and Worms

Ant

Black is his colour
And he comes out of darkness
To a space of light
Where the grass rattles
And the wind booms.

In his home underground
The stones are silent
Roots and seeds make no noise.

Like fine wires
His legs tremble
Over the ground.
Raindrops hiss and explode
Around him
But he runs zig-zagging
From their cold touch.

At last one raindrop,
Bright balloon of water,
Bursts on his back
Becoming his own flood.
Frantic, he spins,
Finds ground again, and scurries
Towards some crack in an enormous Ark.

ZOË BAILEY

Dragonfly

Over the pond
where the children play
I saw somebody
strange, today:
a slender, glittering,
trembling thing
with stuff like cellophane
on its wing.

It wasn't a butterfly
or bee
lolloping, blundering
loose and free . . . .
it darted here
and it darted there
like a quivering firework
in the air.

Down by the pond
I stared, and stood
in the heat of the morning.
I wished it would
stay and settle,
but it went by,
burning, beautiful
dragonfly.

JEAN KENWARD

Spider

Fastening his lifeline to the edge
Of the perilous ledge,
He scrambles down the vertical cliff face
Of infinite giddy space,
And paying out the ladder
Coiled in his dusty bladder
Falls head-first with waving hands,
The wizard of his miniature trapeze.
Now for a moment on the air he stands
Miraculously poised until he sees
Some menace hover near; then quiet and quick
This nimble Indian does his old rope trick.

BASIL DOWLING

Poetry Close-up

1. Why does Carl Sandburg call his poem 'Worms and the Wind'?

   Having read this poem carefully, can you now imagine and write your own conversation between two worms?

2. In which season does Douglas Gibson's poem 'Bumble-Bee' take place?

3. What is the land of 'hairgrass and hollows' in the poem by Clive Sansom?

4. Why are the gnats 'soon for human body bound' in Odette Tchernine's poem?

   Why do the gnats look like they are performing a ballet?

5. Jean Kenward says the dragonfly has 'stuff like cellophane' on its wing. Can you explain this?

6. What is the spider doing in the poem by Basil Dowling?

7. From the poems, choose words which best describe movement.

Other Things To Do

1. Find out about the insects that lived millions of years ago.

2. What is a slow-worm?

3. Insecticides are in common use today on farms. Are there any disadvantages in using these chemicals?

4. Draw a detailed diagram of an insect's body and describe it. Explain why a spider is not an insect.

Fish and Water Creatures

"Tadpoles are fat brown dots
That stand on their tails to nibble weed"

In this section, you will find some poets' thoughts on creatures which spend all, or most of their time, in the water. Read the poems and then think about these questions.

Can you imagine what it's like under water?

.... Think of —a cool green world .... waving fronds .... rippling currents .... menacing rocks .... deep, black depths.

.... Think of —shining silver scales .... quivering fins .... unwinking eyes .... quick, darting movements .... shimmering colours .... snapping jaws.

Some of these creatures can be found on the land. How can we describe them?

.... Think of —scuttling crabs .... lumbering walrus .... crawling turtles .... sliding seals .... basking crocodiles.

If you wish to write your own poem, these words may help you.

sparkle	scum	algae	predator	shoal	shallow
plunge	gloomy	display	school	shimmer	dank
emerald	slimy	pollution	spawn	chill	froth
stagnant	stickleback	swirl	tentacles	flippers	

In The Swim

There are many different kinds of creatures which spend some or all of their life in the water.
Here are three examples: frog; whale; salmon.

Draw each one and write its life history including —
.... where it lives .... how long it lives .... what it eats
.... how it breathes .... the dangers it faces.

If you turn to page 53 you will find some questions on the poems and some more things to do.

47

Tadpoles

Tadpoles are fat brown dots
That stand on their tails to nibble weed
Or swish them from side to side
To drive to places to feed:
A head with a tail
Waiting till the body comes,
Waiting for legs
To make it a frog
That climbs from the water on to a stone
And bounces slowly away to a life of its own.

STANLEY COOK

Frogs

Frogs sit more solid
Than anything sits. In mid-leap they are
Parachutists falling
In a free fall. They die on roads
With arms across their chests and
Heads high.

I love frogs that sit
Like Buddha, that fall without
Parachutes, that die
Like Italian tenors.

Above all, I love them because,
Pursued in water,
They never
Panic so much that they fail
To make stylish triangles
With their ballet dancer's
Legs.

NORMAN MacCAIG

Tiddlers

Here where the road now runs to Aberdare
the old canal lay stagnant in its bed
of reeds and rushes housing dragonflies
which flashed from sunshine into willow shade.

Beneath this very bridge we came to fish
for roach and perch and other smaller fry
like minnows, sticklebacks and tiny frogs
and all these smelt peculiarly of pits.

A smell of stinkhorn-fungus, coal and damp
still clung to them as though they had swum up
some subterranean passage from the mine.

They smelt the house out when we got them home
and, when we changed the water, always died:
clean water killed them.

TOM EARLEY

Goldfish

Orange shapes
Dart to and fro,
Going up for food
Then diving down below.

Tails flap
Side by side,
Gills open
Bubbles rise.

Round and through
The weed they go,
Darting with sudden move
Then still and slow.

RUSSELL HOWELL

The Shark

A treacherous monster is the Shark,
He never makes the least remark.

And when he sees you on the sand,
He doesn't seem to want to land.

He watches you take off your clothes,
And not the least excitement shows.

His eyes do not grow bright or roll,
He has astounding self-control.

He waits till you are quite undrest,
And seems to take no interest.

And when towards the sea you leap,
He looks as if he were asleep.

But when you once get in his range,
His whole demeanour seems to change.

He throws his body right about,
And his true character comes out.

It's no use crying or appealing,
He seems to lose all decent feeling.

After this warning you will wish
To keep clear of this treacherous fish.

His back is black, his stomach white,
He has a very dangerous bite.

LORD ALFRED DOUGLAS

Dolphins

The dolphins play in the sea like children,
Diving, leaping ahead of the long ship,
Rising out of the sparkling waves.
   Their jaws smile,
    "Friends," they seem to say,
    "We are friends; play with us."

The water sprays from their curving backs,
And in the bubbles of their shining wake
   Small fish watch the game
   Round-eyed and
   Open-mouthed.

However fast the ship, the dolphins are faster,
Sliding joyfully through the emerald sea;
At last, descending into the deepest water,
They swim away from the ship and the bright sky.

ZOË BAILEY

Otter

Sun-flickery
in his coat of many bubbles
he melts into water,
seldom troubles to rise for air,
an oil-slickery streak
of brilliantine, there
below the surface:
a shimmer below the glimmer
and spangle of summer,
a swirl with a tail,
a stain, a shadow
oil-slickery in his trickery
of dodges and feints
and dives and bubbly delvings.

Yet in the field all yikkery
he lolloped, less than a dog,
lay like a rough old log
in the sun, dry as a stick;
and I ached to toss him in the pool,
to see him wed to water,
doing his sleekings, slick,
to his own satisfaction
in dark liquefaction.

BRIAN CARTER

Seal

See how he dives
From rocks with a zoom!
See how he darts
Through his watery room
Past crabs and eels
And green seaweed,
Past fluffs of sandy
Minnow feed!
See how he swims
With a swerve and a twist,
A flip of the flipper,
A flick of the wrist!
Quicksilver-quick,
Softer than spray,
Down he plunges
And sweeps away;
Before you can think,
Before you can utter
Words like 'Dill pickle'
Or 'Apple butter',
Back up he swims
Past sting-ray and shark,
Out with a zoom,
A whoop, a bark;
Before you can say
Whatever you wish,
He plops at your side
With a mouthful of fish!

WILLIAM JAY SMITH

Poetry Close-up

1. In the poem called 'Frogs', why does Norman MacCaig say that they sit like Buddha?

2. Read the poem 'Tiddlers' by Tom Earley.
   a) What does he mean when he says the canal is stagnant?
   b) Can you find out what stinkhorn-fungus is?
   c) Why do you think clean water killed the tiddlers?

3. Read Russell Howell's poem about goldfish.
   a) What are gills?
   b) Why do the bubbles rise?

4. What does Zoë Bailey mean by 'their shining wake' in her poem about dolphins?

5. Brian Carter has written a poem about an otter. Why does it have a 'coat of many bubbles'?

   In the same poem, the otter is described in water and on land. Where does he look best? Why?

6. Imagine you are a fish. Describe how you feel when a fisherman tries to catch you and nearly succeeds.

Other Things To Do

1. Watery places can be dangerous. Write a list of rules we should keep when we are near a canal, on a river bank or at the seaside.

2. Find out all you can about shellfish. Can you make a collection of shells?

3. Much of our food comes from the water. Read some books about fishing and find out about — trawling .... the purse seine net .... the drift net .... fish farms .... tuna fishing .... fly fishing .... whaling.

Dogs

"Asleep he wheezes at his ease.
He only wakes to scratch his fleas."

In this section, you will find some poets' thoughts on dogs. Read the poems, then think about these questions on man's best friend.

How do dogs behave?

.... Think of —yapping pekinese .... busy terriers
.... trotting dachshunds .... friendly
mongrels.

.... Think of —pulling and panting .... walking at
heel .... jumping up with wet paws
.... scampering round the garden ....
sniffing and growling.

How do dogs help us?

.... Think of —a farmer and his sheepdog ....
a policeman and his alsation ....
a huntsman and his hounds .... a guide
dog and his master .... an Eskimo and
his huskies.

If you wish to write your own poem, these words may help you.

train	nuisance	expression	lively	tiny	noisy
scent	howl	fetch	pounce	lick	loyal
cower	cringe	worry	pads	fierce	bound
coax	obedient	stray	trust	praise	coat

All Sorts of Dogs

Some animals in the dog family are still very wild.
These include the — wolf; fox; dingo; hyena; jackal.
You could find out as much as you can about each
of them.

There are many stories about famous dogs.
Can you discover more about these dogs —
Greyfriars Bobby; Laika; Rin Tin Tin; Gelert; Lassie?

If you turn to page 59 you will find some questions
on the poems themselves and some more things to do.

The Hairy Dog

My dog's so furry I've not seen
His face for years and years:
His eyes are buried out of sight,
I only guess his ears.

When people ask me for his breed,
I do not know or care:
He has the beauty of them all
Hidden beneath his hair.

HERBERT ASQUITH

Lone Dog

I'm a lean dog, a keen dog, a wild dog and lone,
I'm a rough dog, a tough dog, hunting on my own!
I'm a bad dog, a mad dog, teasing silly sheep;
I love to sit and bay the moon and keep fat souls from
    sleep.

I'll never be a lap dog, licking dirty feet,
A sleek dog, a meek dog, cringing for my meat.
Not for me the fireside, the well-filled plate,
But shut door and sharp stone and cuff and kick and
    hate.

Not for me the other dogs, running by my side,
Some have run a short while, but none of them would
    bide.
O mine is still the lone trail, the hard trail, the best,
Wide wind and wild stars and the hunger of the quest.

IRENE McLEOD

Dogs

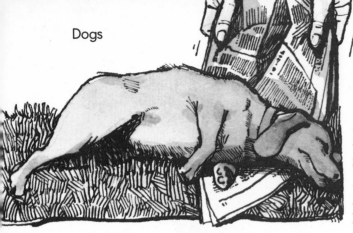

Roger the Dog

Asleep he wheezes at his ease.
He only wakes to scratch his fleas.

He hogs the fire, he bakes his head
As if it were a loaf of bread.

He's just a sack of snoring dog.
You can lug him like a log.

You can roll him with your foot,
He'll stay snoring where he's put.

I take him out for exercise,
He rolls in cowclap up to his eyes.

He will not race, he will not romp,
He saves his strength for gobble and chomp.

He'll work as hard as you could wish
Emptying his dinner dish,

Then flops flat, and digs down deep,
Like a miner, into sleep.

TED HUGHES

Bad Dog

All day long, Bones hasn't been seen
— But now he comes slinking home
Smelling of ditches and streams
And pastures and pinewoods and loam
And tries to crawl under my bed.
His coat is caked with mud,
And one of his ears drips blood.
Nobody knows where he's been.

'Who did it?' they ask him, 'who ....?
He'll have to be bathed .... the sinner ....
Pack him off to his basket ....
You *bad dog*, you'll get no dinner ....'
And he cowers, and rolls an eye.
Tomorrow, I *won't* let him go —
But he licks my hand, and then — oh,
How I wish that I had been too.

BRIAN LEE

My Puppy

It's funny
my puppy
knows just how I feel.

When I'm happy
he's yappy
and squirms like an eel.

When I'm grumpy
he's slumpy
and stays at my heel.

It's funny
my puppy
knows such a great deal.

AILEEN FISHER

Greedy Dog

This dog will eat anything.

Apple cores and bacon fat,
Milk you poured out for the cat.
He likes the string that ties the roast
And relishes hot buttered toast.
Hide your chocolates! He's a thief,
He'll even eat your handkerchief.
And if you don't like sudden shocks,
Carefully conceal your socks.
Leave some soup without a lid,
And you'll wish you never did.
When you think he must be full,
You find him gobbling bits of wool,
Orange peel or paper bags,
Dusters and old cleaning rags.

This dog will eat anything,
Except for mushrooms and cucumber.

Now what is wrong with those, I wonder?

JAMES HURLEY

Full Circle

When John was ten they gave the boy
(A farmer's son) no passing toy,
But his own sheep-dog, eight weeks old.
They'd play round barn and rick and fold
Till running, John would turn to find
His puppy sitting far behind.
With puzzled look and whimpers he
Would plead, "O master, wait for me!"

The years sped on. Through wind and weather
The boy and dog grew up together.
On hill and dale, through heath and fern,
Nor did John need to slow and turn.
When rounding sheep the dog roamed wide
Outstripping far his master's stride;
He'd work the flock, his joy — his pride —
With whistles only as a guide.

And twelve years on the dog was still
A close companion on the hill,
But in the truck he'd often stay
And guard the gear. Now growing grey
In cheek and muzzle, when again
They strolled together down the lane,
He'd pant and pause, and sightless he
Would plead, "O master, wait for me!"

RUTH SKILLING

Poetry Close-up

1. Can you guess the breed of 'The Hairy Dog'?

2. In the poem 'Lone Dog' by Irene McLeod, what does the dog enjoy doing that farmers would not like?

3. Read the poem 'Roger the Dog' by Ted Hughes. Which two things does Roger enjoy most?

4. In the poem 'My Puppy', how does the dog behave when the writer is happy?

5. From the poem 'Greedy Dog', list all the items of food eaten by the dog.

6. Read the poem 'Full Circle' by Ruth Skilling.
   a) How were instructions given to the dog working the sheep?
   b) The end of the poem is quite sad. Why?

7. Imagine your dog helps to rescue you from danger. Write the story of what happened.

Other Things To Do

1. What is a veterinary surgeon and what does he do? Find the name and opening times of your nearest vet.

2. Draw the cartoon dogs 'Pluto' and 'Snoopy'.

3. Can you find out how police dogs are trained and used?

4. Find out and write about guide dogs for the blind.

5. List six common breeds of dog. Draw and colour them. Then write about your own favourite breed.

Cats

"Cats sleep
Anywhere,
Any table,
Any chair"

In this section, you will find some poets' thoughts on cats. Read the poems and think about these questions.

What are cats like?

.... Think of —agile bodies .... arched backs .... slit-like eyes .... stealthy movements .... enormous leaps .... hissing and scratching .... purring and rubbing.

How do they behave around the house?

.... Think of —cats and .... window sills .... fireside rugs .... sunny corners .... wicker baskets.

... Think of —cats and .... playing games .... chasing tails .... pulling wool .... turning somersaults .... catching mice .... stalking birds.

If you wish to write your own poem, these words may help you.

luxurious	stretch	exotic	stare	feline	superior
serene	content	silky	creep	lazy	groom
graceful	independent	spring	sleek	curl	pounce
supple	agile	delicate	bushy	fluffy	soft

Cats Corner

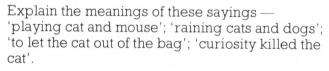

Explain the meanings of these sayings — 'playing cat and mouse'; 'raining cats and dogs'; 'to let the cat out of the bag'; 'curiosity killed the cat'.

Write about (a) a cat burglar;
(b) the cat-o'-nine-tails.

Make a list of wild cats and write about them.

If you turn to page 66 you will find some questions on the poems themselves and some more things to do.

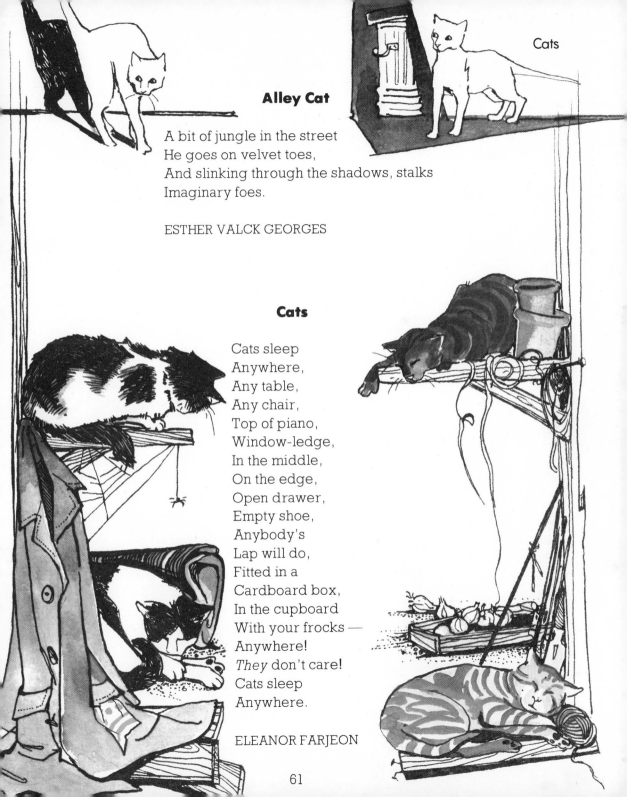

Alley Cat

A bit of jungle in the street
He goes on velvet toes,
And slinking through the shadows, stalks
Imaginary foes.

ESTHER VALCK GEORGES

Cats

Cats sleep
Anywhere,
Any table,
Any chair,
Top of piano,
Window-ledge,
In the middle,
On the edge,
Open drawer,
Empty shoe,
Anybody's
Lap will do,
Fitted in a
Cardboard box,
In the cupboard
With your frocks —
Anywhere!
They don't care!
Cats sleep
Anywhere.

ELEANOR FARJEON

Cats

Cat

The black cat yawns,
Opens her jaws,
Stretches her legs,
And shows her claws.

Then she gets up
And stands on four
Long stiff legs
And yawns some more.

She shows her sharp teeth,
She stretches her lip,
Her slice of a tongue
Turns up at the tip.

Lifting herself
On her delicate toes,
She arches her back
As high as it goes.

She lets herself down
With particular care,
And pads away
With her tail in the air.

MARY BRITTON MILLER

Yellow Cat

'There he is,' yells Father,
Grabbing lumps of soil,
'That yellow tabby's on the fence.
Drown him in boiling oil.
He's scratching at my runner beans.
Bang at the window, quick.
Wait till I get my laces done
I'll beat him with my stick.'

'Too late,' they shout, 'he's on the fence.
He's turning, Father, wait.'
'I'll give him turning, I'll be there,
I'll serve him on a plate.'

They banged the window, Father stormed
And hopped with wild despair;
The cat grew fat with insolence
And froze into a stare.
Its brazen glare stopped Father
With its blazing yellow light;
The silken shape turned slowly
And dropped gently out of sight.

GREGORY HARRISON

Fat Cat

Siamese have cobalt eyes, their tails are thin and
   kinky,
Siamese are slender, Siamese are slinky,
The experts are agreed on that —
They haven't seen this family cat.

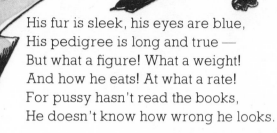

His fur is sleek, his eyes are blue,
His pedigree is long and true —
But what a figure! What a weight!
And how he eats! At what a rate!
For pussy hasn't read the books,
He doesn't know how wrong he looks.

Left-over yogurt, frozen peas,
Spaghetti, any kind of cheese,
He wolfs them down (if that's the word)
Then ups and outs and grabs a bird.
He sits below the baby's chair
To catch the dropped bits in the air,
The phone rings and you turn your back,
He's on the table, snicker snack.

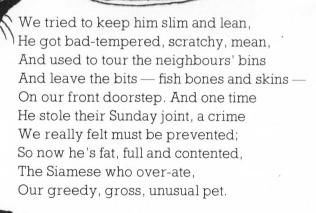

We tried to keep him slim and lean,
He got bad-tempered, scratchy, mean,
And used to tour the neighbours' bins
And leave the bits — fish bones and skins —
On our front doorstep. And one time
He stole their Sunday joint, a crime
We really felt must be prevented;
So now he's fat, full and contented,
The Siamese who over-ate,
Our greedy, gross, unusual pet.

MARY RAYNER

The Tom-Cat

At midnight in the alley
A Tom-cat comes to wail,
And he chants the hate of a million years
As he swings his snaky tail.

Malevolent, bony, brindled,
Tiger and devil and bard,
His eyes are coals from the middle of Hell
And his heart is black and hard.

He twists and crouches and capers
And bares his curved sharp claws,
And he sings to the stars of the jungle nights,
Ere cities were, or laws.

Beast from a world primeval,
He and his leaping clan,
When the blotched red moon leers over the roofs,
Give voice to their scorn of man.

He will lie on a rug tomorrow
And lick his silky fur,
And veil the brute in his yellow eyes
And play he's tame, and purr.

But at midnight in the alley
He will crouch again and wail,
And beat the time for his demon's song,
With the swing of his demon's tail.

DON MARQUIS

The Stray Cat

It's just an old alley cat
that has followed us all the way home.

It hasn't a star on its forehead,
or a silky satiny coat.

No proud tiger stripes, no dainty tread,
no elegant velvet throat.

It's a splotchy, blotchy
city cat, not pretty cat,
a rough little tough little bag of old bones.

"Beauty," we shall call you.
"Beauty, come in."

EVE MERRIAM

On a Cat, Ageing

He blinks upon the hearth-rug,
   And yawns in deep content,
Accepting all the comforts
   That Providence has sent.

Louder he purrs and louder,
   In one glad hymn of praise
For all the night's adventures,
   For quiet restful days.

Life will go on for ever,
   With all that cat can wish;
Warmth and the glad procession
   Of fish and milk and fish.

Only — the thought disturbs him —
   He's noticed once or twice,
The times are somehow breeding
   A nimbler race of mice.

ALEXANDER GRAY

Poetry Close-up

1. Read 'Alley Cat' and explain how you think the creature would be acting when stalking 'imaginary foes'.

2. Make a list of all the places where cats sleep in the poem 'Cats' by Eleanor Farjeon.

3. Read the poem 'Cat' by Mary Britton Miller and then write down where you think the cat has been and what it has been doing.

4. Describe the tom-cat's eyes in the poem by Don Marquis.

   In the same poem, which word is used to describe the tom-cat's relations?

5. Read the poems by Eve Merriam and Mary Rayner. What differences can you find between the old alley cat and the pedigree cat?

6. After reading the poems can you write down any differences between cats' behaviour at night and their behaviour during the day?

7. Write a story which explains why 'A Cat's Life is a Hard Life'.

Other Things To Do

1. How does a cat use its whiskers?

2. If you keep a cat, describe how you look after it.

3. Read about the work of the R.S.P.C.A.

4. Make a list of different pedigree cats. Find out where they originate from .... what special markings they have and any other interesting facts about them.

Other Pets

"I had a hippopotamus; I kept him in a shed
And fed him upon vitamins and vegetable bread;"

The poems in this section are about animals kept
as pets. Read the poems and think about these
questions on the animals that live with us.

If you were a pet, what would it be like?

.... Think of —swimming in circles .... being stared
at .... food in plenty .... being
handled by children .... beds of hay
.... living behind bars.

How do different pets behave?

.... Think of —ambling tortoises .... burrowing
gerbils .... nibbling rabbits and
gnawing hamsters .... unwinking fish.

Would an elephant make a good pet?

.... Think of —powerful help .... instant showers ....
large accommodation .... a hearty
appetite .... daily exercise.

If you wish to write your own poem, these words may help you.

friendly	cage	perform	affectionate	curl	preen
playful	straw	frisky	familiar	perch	tropical
clumsy	whiskers	treasured	stroke	beak	foreign
favourite	amuse	fur	swim	feathers	hutch

Pet Parade

Here is a list of some common pets from around the world:

tortoise; budgerigar; gerbil; golden hamster; guinea pig.

Choose three from the list. Draw and write about — the countries they came
from .... how best to look after them .... what they eat and drink .... where we
should keep them.

If you turn to page 74 you will find some questions on the poems themselves
and some more things to do.

Gerbil

Two brown eyes
peep out of the straw,
a quivering nose
and not much more —
a tail as thick
as a bit of string —
he might be a mouse,
or anything.
Tiny, and most
attentive, he
looks as if
he's measuring me.

'Two blue eyes
look into my straw:
arms and legs
and a good deal more;
clumsy and huge,
I wonder why
it grows so wide
and it grows so high?
What a peculiar
voice it's got . . . .
It is a PERSON,
is it not?'

JEAN KENWARD

Goldfish

One small fish in a
Polythene bag;
Can't swim round, can
Only look sad.
Take a pair of scissors,
Snip a quick hole,
Down flops water
And fish into a bowl!

She waits a little moment,
Flips her tail free,
Then off into circles
As frisk as can be.
Dash-about — splash-about —
Do what you wish:
You're mine, you black-spotted
Cheeky-eyed
Fish!

JOHN WALSH

Tortoises

They lumber painfully
on scaly legs,
push out
beneath their lonely shells
grotesque grey necks.
In wrinkled horny skin
ancient eyes blink,
their tiny mouths
silently complain.

DOUGLAS GIBSON

68

Tortoise

Lumbering carefully over stone and earth,
   Edging, stumbling, groping blindly,
To the favourite place of Michaelmas daisies.
   His food finished, now the tortoise
Feels his way one foot after another,
   Choosing a path among the grass,
Which looks like willows hovering high above his hard shell.
   Afternoon appears, sleep overpowers the beast.
Making heavy footsteps the tortoise finds a sleeping-place,
   One eye closes and the scum of the eyelid passes over both eyes,
The tortoise falls into a shelled sleep.
   Dawn; and he trundles off to find food,
He claws his way over the rockery,
   Which appears to him to be like the Andes,
Passing through glades of raspberries;
   And at last he finds his food,
Lettuce!
   Clumsily he opens his leather-hard jaws,
Draws his fire-red tongue out,
   Then, with a churning of cranking and creaking efforts,
He closes his mouth upon the lettuce;
   Tortoise now returns and digs with great speed,
To hide himself from winter.
   The hole dug, he retreats in his creaking wet-covered shell,
To sleep.

DAVID SPEECHLEY

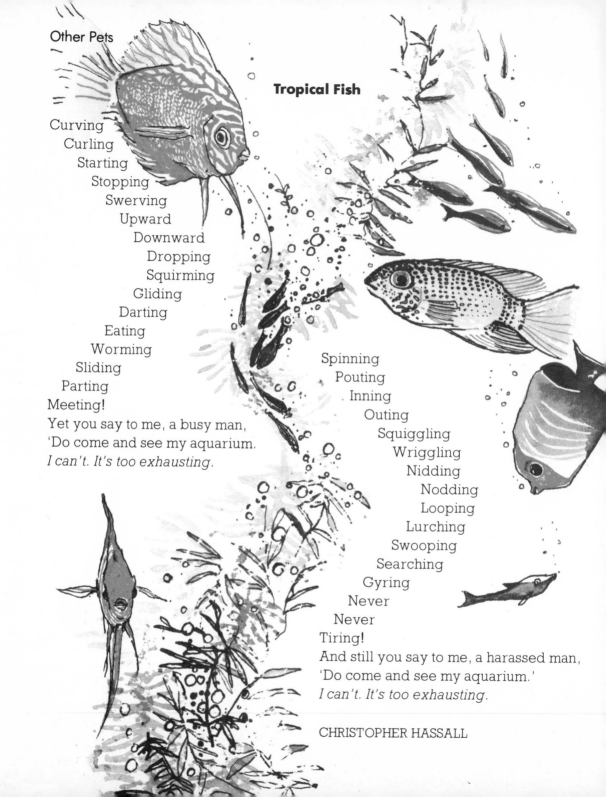

Other Pets

Tropical Fish

Curving
Curling
Starting
Stopping
Swerving
Upward
Downward
Dropping
Squirming
Gliding
Darting
Eating
Worming
Sliding
Parting
Meeting!
Yet you say to me, a busy man,
'Do come and see my aquarium.
I can't. It's too exhausting.

Spinning
Pouting
Inning
Outing
Squiggling
Wriggling
Nidding
Nodding
Looping
Lurching
Swooping
Searching
Gyring
Never
Never
Tiring!
And still you say to me, a harassed man,
'Do come and see my aquarium.'
I can't. It's too exhausting.

CHRISTOPHER HASSALL

from **The Meadow Mouse**

In a shoebox stuffed in an old nylon stocking
Sleeps the baby mouse I found in the meadow,
Where he trembled and shook beneath a stick
Till I caught him up by the tail and brought him in,
Cradled in my hand,

A little quaker, the whole body of him trembling,
His absurd whiskers sticking out like a cartoon mouse,
His feet like small leaves,
Little lizard-feet,
Whitish and spread wide when he tried to struggle away,
Wriggling like a miniscule puppy.

Now he's eaten his three kinds of cheese and drunk from
        his bottle-cap watering trough —

So much he just lies in one corner,
His tail curled under him, his belly big
As his head; his bat-like ears
Twitching, tilting toward the least sound.

Do I imagine he no longer trembles
When I come close to him?
He seems no longer to tremble.

THEODORE ROETHKE

71

I Had a Hippopotamus

I had a hippopotamus; I kept him in a shed
And fed him upon vitamins and vegetable bread;
I made him my companion on many cheery walks,
And had his portrait done by a celebrity in chalks.

His charming eccentricities were known on every side,
The creature's popularity was wonderfully wide;
He frolicked with the Rector in a dozen friendly tussles,
Who could not but remark upon his hippopotamuscles.

If he should be afflicted by depression or the dumps,
By hippopotameasles or the hippopotamumps,
I never knew a particle of peace till it was plain
He was hippopotamasticating properly again.

I had a hippopotamus; I loved him as a friend;
But beautiful relationships are bound to have an end.
Time takes, alas! our joys from us and robs us of our blisses;
My hippopotamus turned out a hippopotamissis.

My housekeeper regarded him with jaundice in her eye;
She did not want a colony of hippopotami;
She borrowed a machine-gun from her soldier-nephew, Percy
And showed my hippopotamus no hippopotamercy.

My house now lacks the glamour that the charming creature gave;
The garage where I kept him is as silent as the grave;
No longer he displays among the motor-tyres and spanners
His hippopotamastery of hippopotamanners.

No longer now he gambols in the orchards in the Spring;
No longer do I lead him through the village on a string;
No longer in the mornings does the neighbourhood rejoice
To his hippopotamusically-modulated voice.

I had a hippopotamus; but nothing upon earth
Is constant in its happiness or lasting in its mirth.
No joy that life can give me can be strong enough to smother
My sorrow for that might-have-been-a-hippopota-mother.

PATRICK BARRINGTON

Poetry Close-up

1. Why does Jean Kenward's gerbil look as if it is 'measuring' her?

2. Where do you think the goldfish came from in John Walsh's poem?

3. Find as many words and phrases as you can from the poem 'Tortoise' by David Speechley which describe how the tortoise moves.

4. After reading the poems by Douglas Gibson and David Speechley, who do you think likes tortoises most? Can you explain why?

5. Why does Christopher Hassall say that watching tropical fish is too exhausting?

6. Theodore Roethke thinks that his meadow mouse no longer trembles. Why do you think he might have stopped?

7. In the poem 'I Had a Hippopotamus', what are 'eccentricities' and a 'celebrity'?

8. Describe a make-believe animal which you think would make the perfect pet.

Other Things To Do

1. Find the names of some of the fish which are kept in an aquarium.

2. Why were canaries used in coal mines?

3. If somebody is used as a guinea pig, what does it mean and where does the saying come from?

4. Some pets in this section are cold blooded and others are warm blooded. Can you find out what these terms mean? Make a list of other animals which fit these headings.

Farm Animals

"The black one, last as usual, swings her head
And coils a black tongue round a grass-tuft."

In this section there are poems about all sorts of farm animals. Read the poems and then think about these questions.

What sorts of sounds might you hear on a farm?

.... Think of —clucking hens .... grunting pigs ....
braying donkeys .... bleating sheep
.... whinnying ponies.

What jobs are there to do on the farm?

.... Think of —milking cows .... feeding pigs ....
collecting eggs .... rounding up and
shearing sheep .... grooming horses
.... lambing time.

Are cattle peaceful creatures?

.... Think of —gentle browsing .... soft lowing ....
big brown eyes.

.... Think of —sharp-horned bulls .... terrifying
snorts .... the ground trembling.

If you wish to write your own poem, these words may help you.

chicken	ungainly	verdant	glossy	stubborn	mane
foal	collie	meadow	supple	thicket	wool
hooves	gambol	neigh	graceful	gallop	elegant
muzzle	frisk	stallion	cud	clumsy	awkward

Farm Facts

— Some cattle are kept for beef and some for milk.
Draw and write about the different breeds of
cattle and what they are used for.

— Find out what you can about leather. Write about
how it is prepared from cow-hide.

If you turn to page 80 you will find some questions
on the poems themselves and some more things to do.

Fetching Cows

The black one, last as usual, swings her head
And coils a black tongue round a grass-tuft. I
Watch her soft weight come down, her split feet spread.

In front, the others swing and slouch; they roll
Their great Greek eyes and breathe out milky gusts
From muzzles black and shiny as wet coal.

The collie trots, at my heels, then plops
Into the ditch. The sea makes a tired sound
That's always stopping though it never stops.

A haycart squats prickeared against the sky,
Hay breath and milk breath. Far out in the West
The wrecked sun founders though its colours fly.

The collie's bored. There's nothing to control . . . .
The black cow is two native carriers
Bringing its belly home, slung from a pole.

NORMAN MacCAIG

Cow

You wouldn't think so solid an animal could be so learned.
You wouldn't think my big empty eyes could understand so much.
You wouldn't think my slow ways could hide such rapid thinking.
You wouldn't think my voice could express wonderful thoughts if it wanted to.
You wouldn't think I was ever planning things while I was chewing,
would you?

Look out for yourselves, I am simply waiting my time.   ALAN BROWNJOHN

Black Lamb

All legs, tight curls of wool,
  A raucous bleat,
He staggers to his mother's
  Milky teat.

And as he sucks,
  His infant tail awry
Records the rhythm
  Of a lamb gone dry.

ELEANOR GLENN WALLIS

The Hens

The night was coming very fast;
It reached the gate as I ran past.

The pigeons had gone to the tower of the church
And all the hens were on their perch,

Up in the barn, and I thought I heard
A piece of a little purring word.

I stopped inside, waiting and staying,
To try to hear what the hens were saying.

They were asking something, that was plain,
Asking it over and over again.

One of them moved and turned around,
Her feathers made a ruffled sound,

A ruffled sound, like a bushful of birds,
And she said her little asking words.

She pushed her head close into her wing,
But nothing answered anything.

ELIZABETH MADOX ROBERTS

Dobbin

The old horse, Dobbin,
  Out at grass
Turns his tail
  To the winds that pass;

And stares at the white road
  Winding down
Through the dwindling fields
  To the distant town.

He hears in the distance,
  A snip-snap trot,
He sees his master,
  A small dark dot,

Riding away
  On the smart new mare
That came last month
  From Pulborough Fair.

Dobbin remembers,
  As horses may,
How often he trotted
  That ringing way.

His coat is ragged
  And blown awry.
He droops his head
  And he knows not why.

Something has happened.
  Something has gone,
The world is changing,
  His work is done.

But his old heart aches
  With a heavier load
As he stands and wonders
  And stares at the road.

ALFRED NOYES

The Stallion

A gigantic beauty of a stallion, fresh and responsive to
    caresses,
Head high in the forehead, wide between the ears,
Limbs glossy and supple, tail dusting the ground,
Eyes full of sparkling wickedness, ears finely cut,
    flexible, moving.

His nostrils dilate as my heels embrace him,
His well-built limbs tremble with pleasure as we race
    and return.

WALT WHITMAN

The Donkey

I saw a donkey
One day old,
His head was too big
For his neck to hold;
His legs were shaky
And long and loose,
They rocked and staggered
And weren't much use.

He tried to gambol
And frisk a bit,
But he wasn't quite sure
Of the trick of it.
His queer little coat
Was soft and grey,
And curled at his neck
In a lovely way.

His face was wistful
And left no doubt
That he felt life needed
Some thinking about.
So he blundered round
In venturesome quest,
And then lay flat
On the ground to rest.

He looked so little
And weak and slim,
I prayed the world
Might be good to him.

ANON.

Poetry Close-up

1. Write the last two lines of 'Fetching Cows' in your own words.

    In the same poem, 'a haycart squats prickeared against the sky'. What does this mean?

2. In Alan Brownjohn's poem, what do you think the cow will do when it has finished waiting?

3. Why does Elizabeth Madox Roberts think the hens are asking questions?

4. Why is 'Dobbin' so sad?

5. In 'The Donkey', the poet says the donkey's face is wistful. Do you think the donkey really is feeling this way?

6. The farmer and his family have gone to bed. The animals are planning to run away. Imagine and write down their conversation.

Other Things To Do

1. Write an account of the journey your milk takes from the cow to your table.
    How is milk pasteurised or sterilised?

2. Read and write about how wool has been spun and woven into cloth through the ages.

3. Write about the life of the American cowboy in years gone by.

4. Find out about the very early ancestors of the horse. Draw and write about them.

5. Find out what horsepower is and how it is measured.

6. Read the book 'Black Beauty' by Anna Sewell.

Animals of Make-Believe and Yesteryear

"Along the valley of the Ump
Gallops the fearful Hippocrump."

In this section, you will find some poems about the kind of creatures we never meet. Read the poems and then think about these questions.

How would people feel if they really met a terrifying creature?

.... Think of —hideous, deafening roars .... nostrils flaring wide
.... yellow, glaring eyes .... wicked claws and slavering jaws
.... bloody fangs.

.... Think of —white, trembling faces .... wide staring eyes ....
chattering teeth .... screams of panic .... legs turning to jelly.

Why do some strange creatures make us smile, rather than tremble?

.... Think of —ridiculous shapes .... rubbery teeth
.... revolving eyes .... strange food .... weird sounds
.... peculiar behaviour.

If you wish to write your own poem, these words may help you.

dinosaur	enormous	evil	terrify	mythical	menace
extinct	fierce	horrendous	ghastly	ferocious	attack
incredible	brutal	awe	wonder	massive	awesome
gnash	monstrous	leathery	gigantic	absurd	grotesque

Disappearing Dinosaurs

The most famous extinct animals are dinosaurs.
Find out as much as you can about them.

.... How did life on Earth develop before the dinosaurs lived?

.... Describe the world when the dinosaurs lived; the plants, and the other creatures in the sea and in the air.

.... How did these giant 'lizards' evolve from amphibians and why?

.... Which dinosaurs were 'carnivores' and which were 'herbivores'?

.... For how long did the dinosaurs exist and why did they disappear'?

If you turn to page 88 you will find some questions on the poems themselves and some more things to do.

When Dinosaurs Ruled the Earth

Brontosaurus, diplodocus, gentle trachodon,
Dabbled in the muds of time,
Once upon, upon.

Tyrannosaurus raised his head
And rolled his evil eye,
Bared his long and yellow teeth
And bid his neighbours 'bye.
His pygmy brain was slow to grasp
The happenings of the day
And so he roamed and slew his friends
And ate without delay.

Brontosaurus, diplodocus, gentle trachodon,
Dabbled in the muds of time,
Once upon, upon.

Allosaurus awed his foe,
He awed his friends who passed,
His teeth were made for tearing flesh,
His teeth were made to gnash.
Taller than a building now,
Taller than a tree,
He roamed about the swamp-filled world
And ate his company.

Brontosaurus, diplodocus, gentle trachodon,
Dabbled in the muds of time,
Once upon, upon.

Eaters of their friends and foe
Or dabblers in the slime,
Their pygmy brains were slow to grasp,
Once upon a time.

PATRICIA HUBBELL

The Monster

A monster who lives in Loch Ness
Is ten thousand years old, more or less:
   He's asleep all the time —
   Which is hardly a crime:
If he weren't, we'd be in a mess.

EDWARD LOWBURY

The Abominable Snowman

I've never seen an abominable snowman,
I'm hoping not to see one,
I'm also hoping, if I do,
That it will be a wee one.

OGDEN NASH

The Brontosaurus

The brontosaurus ranged the earth
   Ten million years ago;
He was a beast of monstrous girth
   But very, very slow.

His neck was long, his tail was too,
   His head was very small;
His length (all this, you know, is true,)
   Was sixty feet in all.

And everybody that he met
   He used to terrify
He was so big and ugly, yet
   He wouldn't hurt a fly.

He was a lizard-type, I'm told;
   Ate seaweed, so they say,
Inspiring us, both young and old
   To eat our greens each day.

H. A. C. EVANS

from **The Hippocrump**

Along the valley of the Ump
Gallops the fearful Hippocrump.
His hide is leathery and thick;
His eyelids open with a *Click*!
His mouth he opens with a *Clack*!
He has three humps upon his back;
On each of these there grows a score
Of horny spikes, and sometimes more.
His hair is curly, thick and brown;
Beneath his chin a beard hangs down.
He has eight feet with hideous claws;
His neck is long — and O his jaws!
The boldest falters in his track
To hear those hundred teeth go *Clack*!
The Hippocrump is fierce indeed,
But if he eats the baneful weed
That grows beside the Purple Lake,
His hundred teeth begin to ache.
Then how the creature stamps and roars
Along the Ump's resounding shores!
The drowsy cattle faint with fright;
The birds fall flat, the fish turn white.
Even the rocks begin to shake;
The children in their beds awake;
The old ones quiver, quail, and quake.
'Alas!' they cry. 'Make no mistake,
It is *Himself* — he's got the Ache
From eating by the Purple Lake!'
Some say, 'It is *Old You-know-who* —
He's in a rage: what *shall* we do?' . . . .

JAMES REEVES

Wyvern

All my research has shown
Very little is known
Of the Wyvern or where it inhabits;
One informant insists
That the creature exists
Upon rhubarb, rice pudding and rabbits.

I also have heard
That the Wyvern's a bird
Reminiscent of serpent or snake;
It has two eagle's legs
And it lays speckled eggs
That young ornithologists take.

Of incredible size,
Like a dragon that flies,
With a wing span of twenty-five feet,
The Wyvern is not
Any problem to pot,
And when roasted is pleasant to eat.

Its long-taloned claws
And its slavering jaws
Are features entirely distinct.
Big-game hunters who chase it
Can outwit and outpace it,
And maybe that's why it's extinct!

CHARLES CONNELL

The Dodo

The Dodo used to walk around
And take the sun and air,
The Sun yet warms his native ground —
The Dodo is not there!
That voice which used to squawk and squeak
Is now forever dumb —
Yet you see his bones and beak
All in the Museum.

HILAIRE BELLOC

Werewolf

A Werewolf is just like a wolf —
Long teeth, slavering tongue, bristling hair —
But a wolf can be dated, is easily located,
While a Werewolf is simply not there.

A wolf can be found on the steppes,
Chasing Russian, troika or bear;
But if you're on the track of a Werewolf, alack,
It will drive you to abject despair.

A wolf's a predictable beast;
It proceeds in a certain direction,
While a Werewolf will say, 'I'll be with you to-day',
But it never turns up for inspection.

A wolf feeds whenever it can
On chicken or rabbit or hare;
But a Werewolf, they say, likes to eat twice a day
And prefers human flesh, medium rare.

Some men, when the moon's at the full,
Undergo a complete transformation;
With fierce howls and roars, they run round on all fours,
Killing people without hesitation.

When they turn into Werewolves themselves,
Their nails grow much sharper and longer;
When their palms become hairy, then it's best to be wary,
For the odds are they're now getting stronger.

If ever you meet with a Werewolf,
Remember this piece of advice —
A real silver bullet, fired straight down its gullet,
Will finish it off in a trice.

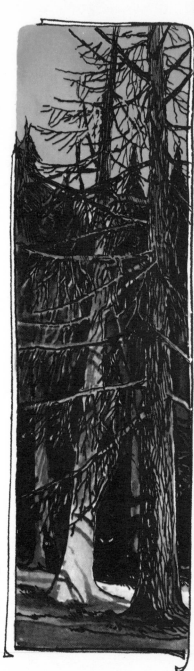

CHARLES CONNELL

The Marrog

My desk's at the back of the class
And nobody nobody knows
I'm a Marrog from Mars
With a body of brass
And seventeen fingers and toes.
Wouldn't they shriek if they knew
I've three eyes at the back of my head
And my hair is bright purple
My nose is deep blue
And my teeth are half yellow half red?
My five arms are silver with knives on them sharper
   than spears.
I could go back right now if I liked —
And return in a million light years.
I could gobble them all for
I'm seven foot tall
And I'm breathing green flames from my ears.
Wouldn't they yell if they knew
If they guessed that a Marrog was here?
Ha-ha they haven't a clue —
Or wouldn't they tremble with fear!
Look, look, a Marrog
They'd all scrum and shout.
The blackboard would fall and the ceiling would
   crack
And the teacher would faint I suppose.
But I grin to myself sitting right at the back
And Nobody nobody knows.

R. C. SCRIVEN

Poetry Close-up

1. Patricia Hubbell writes about the Tyrannosaurus in her poem 'When Dinosaurs Ruled the Earth'. She says that he has a pygmy brain. What does she mean by this?

2. In the poem 'Wyvern', Charles Connell talks about his 'research'. What is meant by this and what is an 'informant'?

   In the same poem, what are 'speckled eggs'? What is an ornithologist?

3. Find out what a 'troika' is. It is mentioned in the poem 'Werewolf'.

4. R.C. Scriven in 'The Marrog' writes about 'light years'. What is a light year?

   The same poet also tells us that 'The Marrog' is sitting in the class-room. Why do you think nobody makes a fuss?

5. Imagine that you travel to the planet of 'The Marrog'. Describe your adventures there.

Other Things To Do

1. Find out as much as you can about both the 'Loch Ness Monster' and the 'Abominable Snowman'. What evidence is there that they exist? Do you believe in them?

2. Many strange animals appear in legends and myths. These are some of them:
   unicorn; centaur; minotaur; gorgon; sphinx; pegasus.

   Find out what you can about these and any other mythical creatures.

3. Make a picture of one of the creatures you have met in this section.